A Break from the Chaos

Part 1

By T.L. Larson

For my wife, Ariane.

My love, my inspiration,

my first and most important fan.

A Break from the Chaos: Part 1

© 2020 Travis Larson

All rights reserved. No portion of this book may be used or reproduced in any form without written permission from the publisher, except in the case of reprints in the context of review or as permitted by U.S. copyright law.

A Healthy Nugget book

Cover by Ariane Larson.

For permissions contact:
Abreakfromthechaos@gmail.com

ISBN: 978-1-7362955-0-2

Table of Contents

1) Preface

2) A break from the chaos.
   - Essence
   - A Break from the Chaos
   - To My Darling
   - The Path Ahead
   - The Desk

3) Seasons bring change... and hardship.
   - A Beautiful Smile... A Beautiful Lie?
   - Season of Reflection
   - The Witching Hour
   - Anything
   - Death's Unfair Choice

4) Repairing the soul.
   - Five Senses of Life
   - Always Be Cool
   - How Can I Help?
   - Shoes for the Soul
   - Memories

5) Just because...
   - Not for the Faint-Hearted
   - Insatiable
   - A Heavy Meal
   - Attention Deficit
   - Where to Begin

Table of Contents

6) Comfort from chaos.
    - Comfort from Chaos
    - Sunny Days
    - Life's Breath
    - The Path to Knowhere
    - The Pebble in My Shoe

7) Blood, guts, and... glory?
    - Chosen
    - Only Human
    - Buried Alive
    - Football
    - Ribs

8) Life can be mean.
    - Insanity
    - Life's Unforgiving Rage
    - Pandemic of Panic
    - Anger Builds
    - Without Pain Would We Know?

9) Guiding others... without a compass.
    - The Gift
    - Sitting on the Beach
    - One Last Time, One More Time
    - The Third Law
    - A Little Less Peanut Butter

Table of Contents

10) Learning to move on.
    - Procrastination
    - Always Tomorrow
    - Acquaintance with Death
    - Posture and Attitude
    - Forward

11) Just for fun.
    - Cursed
    - Drums
    - Grip
    - The Evolution of a Man

12) Goodbye for now...
    - An Incomplete Farewell

Preface

(The boring part only a few of you will read).

I abhorred English class as a kid, and I absolutely could not stand poetry. I didn't understand it, or more simply, I didn't want to understand it. Yet, I still enjoyed reading a good book from time to time. Lord of the Rings, Harry Potter, and quite a bit of Stephen King novels started to fill my shelves. It truly has only been in the past year or so, that I have come to appreciate poetry. I feel I am only beginning to scratch the surface, but now William Carlos Williams, Robert Frost and many others are beginning to take their place in my home.

I have blinked, and I now find myself as a Family Medicine physician. Not quite a well-to-do, distinguished, or even experienced one. No, I'm fresh out of training, just starting life in private practice, and still living paycheck to paycheck in order to pay off an exorbitant amount of debt. In my short time here, I have realized the field of medicine is not made of butterflies, rainbows and unicorns. It has been full of trials and tribulations over the past decade. Stress has become a frequent part of life and can be such a burden. In order to cope with stress, one needs an outlet. To make a long story short, I found this outlet in writing poetry.

My poetry journey started when I happened to stumble across a "creativity in medicine" elective while I was in medical school. I honestly took it mostly as a "blow off" course so I could travel for residency interviews during my 4th year of medical school. I ended up absolutely loving it. I found a new interest in writing that I dabbled in from time to time. Then the beast called "residency" came, and consumed my life. On rare occasions, I had an opportunity where I could stop treading water, resurface, and relax. However, during these breaks I was often so exhausted I just wanted to "vegetate" by sleeping and catching up on TV shows.

At some point I felt myself slipping. Then I started my year as chief resident and the workload only increased. Managing and navigating one mind through residency was tough enough. Suddenly, there was now a responsibility of 30. I found I was in desperate need of this outlet.

Then one day, I happened to pick up a pen. There are particular events, moments, or patients in medicine that really stick with you. An almost PTSD- like fashion occurs, with flashes of these experiences coming and going. While there are plenty of good moments to savor, unfortunately, it's usually the bad moments that tend to hang around the longest. That day, I wrote down one of these haunting experiences. I felt lighter. A piece of me was suddenly more at peace. I followed this feeling throughout my last year in residency and have continued my "therapy" now into my first year of practice. During this time I have continued to write random thoughts, loves, fears, patient encounters, traumatic events, and an occasional random fictional tale.

Despite its hardships, life in medicine has been fantastical, and I am so grateful it has become my profession. The stories and lives you learn about could fill libraries. This little book has a collection of some of my favorite poems that have revealed themselves from my pen and paper over the past year. A majority of these have been influenced by my experiences in medicine in some form or fashion.

Now, before you start tearing them apart in a literary sense... I know these poems are probably not perfect, but humor me and take a peek. I have never considered myself a writer, until recently, and really only an amateur-hobbyist at that. But nonetheless, I hope you will enjoy them. Ahead in these pages are a collection of 50 of my poems from the past year of writing. These are words that found meaning with me, and hopefully will find meaning with you. May they make you laugh, cry, shout, smile, or perhaps feel more whole.

So pull yourself from your chaotic life, this chaotic world, find a place to sit, relax, and take a break with me...

T.L. Larson

A break from the chaos.

1

Essence

Yes, my words bear meaning
    But that is intimate

If my words find meaning with you
    Let it be that

2

A Break from the Chaos

The adventures you'll take me
The people I'll meet
Without ever having to leave my seat

The joys of victory
The heartbreak of loss
Ideas I otherwise would not come across

My attention is yours
Take me away
To another world, but alas I cannot stay…

3

To My Darling

Making the world a lighter place
You care for me when I do not
Sweet caring heart
Darling

Spoken words have never been a strong suit
I cannot seem to express
But I do feel
Deeply

Warmth and happiness when together
Persisting since the beginning
Love flows and follows
Glowing

A long road behind us, the road ahead unknown
Excitement to journey with you
Adventures await
Enchanting

If only a small gesture, I hope you know
You are the reason why
My world, my universe
Everything

4

The Path Ahead

Weary, I finally arrived
At first, unsure if my eyes betrayed me
But the light at the end of the tunnel grew brighter
At last, sweet, fresh air and daylight greeted me.

Leery, I slowly emerged
Accosted by mist of a fog covered valley
Unsure of the terrain ahead
I now sit and ponder.

Query, at the crossroads
Unknowing awaits the path ahead
Will it travel up a mountain of tremendous trials
Or lead down to the river so I may replenish spirit?

Perhaps it would be easiest to just turn back,
But the journey has been too long... Onward!

5
The Desk

A donut, half-eaten
delicately balanced
on a napkin above
the microbe filled surface.

Cold coffee rests,
waiting patiently.
Frozen lunch anxious,
warms too quickly.

Harvested papers
coat the desk,
fallen from a tree
endlessly producing.

Pens lay buried,
occasionally resurfacing.
Others more elusive,
are lost in the fray.

A novel stands
eager to be read,
knowing it may never
leave its post.

Seasons bring change... and hardship.

6

A Beautiful Smile... A Beautiful Lie?

A smile...

So simple
So complex

Brings comfort
Brings joy

Hides truth
Hides pain

Treats sorrow
Treats pain

Spreads lies
Spreads life

A smile.

7

Season of Reflection

The sun shined
and the water gleamed.
I heard a chime in the distance
while the wind blew.
The evergreens swayed
on this hot, Summer day.

The sun hid
and the water froze.
Silence filled the air for miles
while the wind stood still.
The evergreens stayed
on this cold, Winter day.

8
The Witching Hour

Every morning when the clock strikes three,
I guarantee, you will find me…
Awoken by an unknown force.
Restless, unable to change course.

The air crisp, unsettlingly chilling.
Myself and the wind only stirring.
Bullying thoughts now reign king.
Prohibiting hope returning.

A strong empty presence haunts.
My thoughts continue their taunts.
Tossing and turning there is no comfort.
Day wasted if no return to slumber.

No ghosts, witches, or demons to scare me,
but clawing at the floorboards awaits…
                              persistent reality.

9

Anything

Help me...
As I lay here
Drowning in thoughts

Something extraordinary
Something ordinary
Something...

10

Death's Unfair Choice

All eyes fall on me
A table divides the room
Full of family
Myself not belonging

No answers to give
No knowledge to pass on
Nothing left to do
But one decision remains

The room awaits
Already knowing her fate
One decision remains
But no one wishes to make

All eyes now on him
Can't let go
Won't let go
One decision remains

Her body a shell
Only an empty husk
Soul moved on
We can only hope

Laying there lifeless
Heart still beating
Machine breathing
One decision remains

Her suffering continues
Their suffering continues
My suffering continues
One decision remains

The cruelest reality
A recognition of truth
Hope lost, but able to move on
A decision is made

Rest.

T.L. Larson

Repairing the soul.

11

Five Senses of Life

Take a second to breathe
slowly and deeply, take in the scents
cascading through the air.
Life sustaining.

Cease the monotony to taste
striking flavors of spices warm
the soul, as nectars bring comfort.
Savor existence.

Pause the distractions to hear
the beauty of silence, and attend
the performance that surrounds.
Melodious humility.

Stop for an instant to feel
the textures of the world,
embrace, and let them touch back.
Grasp vitality.

Break for a moment to see
various shades embellish and illuminate,
displaying the colors of life.
Heavenly creation.

12

Always Be Cool

      Calm

      Collected

      Confident

      Composed

      Competent

      Considerate

      Curious

      ~~Compassionate~~

          Kind

13
How Can I Help?

She came to me
Life in disarray
Family problems, divorce
Stress, Anxiety

"My daughter hates me."
Depression.

How can I help?

She came to me
Life in chaos
A new diagnosis
Cancer.

"Am I going to die?"
Depression worsens

How can I help?

She came to me
Life in uncertainty
Chemo wreaks havoc
Nausea, vomiting, hair loss, fatigue

"I'm sick, but trying."
An uncertain prognosis

How can I help?

She came to me
Life in mending
A daughter who cares
Feeling loved, feeling supported

"I think I'm going to make it."
A finish line in sight

How can I help?

She came to me
"How can I help?"

A desire to aid others
Admiration grows
A woman who came in pieces
Now built stronger than before

How can I help?

14

Shoes for the Soul

A pair of shoes
discount pair

but they were new
and they were his

most valuable possession
offered the value of protection

"Love the new kicks!"
meant the world.

15
Memories

I spent tonight amongst family, reliving
the past and planning our futures. All while
I remembered those who have come into my life.
I could tell their stories
for days, for all would listen. Who could resist
the drama of life and death?
But instead, let them sleep.
Safe inside the library
between my ears.

T.L. Larson

Just because…

16
Not for the Faint-Hearted

There once was a man
A quite lonely man
Who quite frankly went insane
Even though not a soul heard him complain

It happened late one night
Oh, it was quite a fright
Yes, indeed it was insanity
Oh my… the humanity

He sat quietly in his study
When this unwanted visitor came by
Suddenly at the window… click-clack!
Nearly gave his heart attack

At first there was nothing
Just a bush outside brushing
But as he stared into the darkness
He felt the stare of something heartless

The house suddenly so bare and lonesome
Finding himself alone so loathsome
Each click and creak of the house
Speeding his heart to that of a mouse

As he began to shrug off this sensation
His fears began their mutation
In a manner so very stark
It emerged out of the dark

The fiend taking up the whole frame
At first only thinking it were a game
But those glowing red eyes
Gave him quite the surprise

A wicked smile stretched wide
As the monster lingered outside
His heart returned to a loud drum
For malicious intent could only come

And what happened next
I could not create into text
I could not even get started
For it is not for the faint-hearted...

17
Insatiable

I do not wish fame,
I do not wish fortune,
but I'll graciously take all I can get.

The fanciest cars,
the finest cigars,
but I'll never be in too deep.

Indulge the wanderlust,
travel the world,
but I'll never know who I am.

For what others see,
is what I will be,
just for the sake of more.

18
A Heavy Meal

A meal consumed
Inner rumblings
Uncomfortable bloating

The pressure builds
Inner turmoil
Uncertainty expanding

Release
Relent
Relief!

19
Attention Deficit

Focus.
Attention.
Retention.

Seconds...
minutes...
feels like hours.
Exhausted, distraction settles in.

Sounds important.
What did he say?
Head nods
Any questions?
I don't know...
What to ask?

This chair uncomfortable
My mind impenetrable

Who plays tonight?
Geez these lights are bright.
Man, it would be great to go hiking.
I wonder what it was like to be a Viking?
Oh yeah! That should be a good game.
Ooh I need to pay attention to this frame.

Shoot! I need to pay bills
And pick up milk
And mow the lawn
And read that paper
And call home
And...

How much longer?
My will no stronger.

The clock unmoved, but not disregarded.
Mental notes linger, but soon discarded.

Ugh, I'm not gonna make it...
Just gonna have to fake it.

20
Where to Begin

I wasn't sure where to start
So I started in the middle

Just in case
I need to go back to fix the beginning

And because
I'm not sure how it should end...

Comfort from chaos.

21

Comfort from Chaos

These have been weird times.
Days seem to move slower.
It was a wet Winter,
and it's been a dry Spring.

There is less work to do here,
as we hunker down in our homes.
Trying to avoid exposure.
Hiding from the invisible killer.

Other places are scrambling,
as pandemic rules the land.
Trying to temper the flames.
Facing the monster head on.

At work, stress remains pressing,
as we don't want to be exposed.
At home, a peaceful, but unsettling presence stays.
Perhaps the calm before the storm.

Another restless night.
I had finally slipped off to dream,
but was awoken by the dog.
Perhaps knowing a storm approached.

Thunder rolled in the distance,
as the other storm lie on the horizon.
I laid awake wondering when it would come,
and the storm moved closer.

Rumbling turned to booming crashes,
accompanied by bright flashes.
Wind thrashed the bushes and trees just outside,
while a heavy downpour cleansed Spring's pollen coating.

There I laid wondering,
When would this storm approach?
But comforted by the chaos,
I was able to sleep.

22

Sunny Days

Oh sunny days,
are on their way!
The cold of yesterday
to the warmth of tomorrow.

Oh sunny days,
I cannot wait!
For the long dark days
to forever stay away.

Oh sunny days,
I look for thee!
A glimpse of the sun arising,
the edge of tomorrow emerges.

23

Life's Breath

Life's breath enters in our first few seconds
Leaves us in our last

But there are so many moments
It enters within us

Taken for granted so often
Admired frequently when too late

Breathe
Enjoy Life

24
The Path to Knowhere

The room remains a dark abyss,
but I see a doorway
soon to be outlined by glimpses of morning light.
Something blocks my path just out of sight.

I see the doorway,
but remain unable to navigate the darkness.
A way out... or at least the only way I know.
How do I get there? Will you show...?

I see the doorway.
The path still foreign, but visible.
As the time passes, I see a little more clearly.
Do I have the luxury to wait, as life passes so dearly?

I see the doorway.
Shifting shapes of shadows just beyond.
Something waits for me on the other side.
If I pass through, will truth be verified?

25
The Pebble in My Shoe

To the rock in my life.

You are my rock
Solid, you keep us grounded
Affection not needing confirmation
Our love, an immovable foundation
You keep me sane
You help me when I'm in pain
Even though at times...
You can be a pebble in my shoe

I've never met someone who could talk as much as you
I've never met someone who feels emotion as much as you
You bring so much joy,
But sometimes you really can annoy
Indeed, sometimes....
You can be quite the pebble in my shoe

But...
I've never met someone who could laugh as much as you
And...
I've never met someone who truly loves as much as you

So...
You can stay the pebble in my shoe
In fact...
I hope you always do.

Blood, guts, and... glory?

26

Chosen

So they say
Oh the places you'll go!
Oh the people you'll know!

To the city
To the sky
The only place you'll go is high!

They failed to mention
The road ahead is seldom easy
The road ahead unknown

Yet, you will find the way!
You will find a way!
There must be light on the other side

Will you show me?
Will you guide me?
I can only hope.

27

Only Human

Perfection.
Does it exist?
While searching for it, one can be lost.
But without trying, can anyone be found?

I find myself too often striving for perfection,
And if aiming for perfection one must realize...
Few things in this world are perfect.
In fact, is anything in this world perfect?

When I reach for perfection
Am I ever truly satisfied?
One could drive themselves mad
Making Perfect the enemy of Good.

Sometimes if we could only realize
That we are only human.
Sometimes if I could only realize
That I am only human.

28
Buried Alive

A journey ended
A journey begun
Bright-eyed and bushy-tailed
A whole new world unveiled

Been taught the knowledge
Been taught to care
A future paid for
But no one let the buyer beware

Here is your shovel
Start the digging
Make it six feet deep
Without knowing what I'm committing

Almost done with the digging
Who are we burying?
I'm ready to care
I'm ready to give

Dirt hits my face
Still standing in place
Wait for me to finish...
Wait for me to get out...

No time.
Stay down.
Keep digging.
Head down.

My questions unanswered
My thoughts turn to guilt
Once broken down
Can we be rebuilt?

Nowhere to go
Guilt turns to fear… to crushing anxiety
Only keep digging
For the good of society

Dirt continues to pile in
Frustration now settles in
Is this my fault?
Maybe I can still get out?

Keep digging they say
As dirt turns to wet concrete
Still time to slosh around
Can we change this hardened ground?

Dirt and stone begin to mix
Perhaps I am too broken to fix?
Left here to be brave
As I stand in my own grave

My final thoughts begin to surface
As the light begins to fade
How can I help the others
If I cannot be saved?

29
Football

On occasion,
I'll enjoy a good football game
I admire the determination of athletes and fans alike
It does stir up quite the energy

The roar of a crowd
The raise of a fist
The crack of a beer
All could bring a hearty smile

But never would I have thought
that football allegiances,
could possibly determine…
how well one could doctor.

30
Ribs

An elderly man
Alive, but complex
Awake one second
Gone the next

Thin, cachectic
Mind afar
Some discussion
But no DNR

No pulse, no rhythm
Team rushes to him

Full court press
Start the session
No pulse, no rhythm
Start compression

No pulse, no rhythm
Compression… pads… compression

The initial break
Beneath my hands
Would not matter
If best laid plans

Family is notified
Please do it all
Compressions continue
My skin begins to crawl

Arms are tiring
Time to switch
Next jumps on
Without a hitch

No pulse, no rhythm
Continue work on him

The piston fires
No choice but crush
Compressions continue
Chest cavity now mush

I press and I press
Meeting no resistance
When suddenly… A pulse, a rhythm
Comes to existence

To our horror?
This pulse returned
Please do everything
Family so concerned

A Break from the Chaos

Family is updated
Patient now intubated, sedated
We will be there soon
Hopeful thoughts inundated

A moment of respite
Shattered by alarm
No pulse, no rhythm
Here comes more harm

The beating continues
Compressions restarted
His body's appearance
Not for the faint-hearted

Bruising and bloating
Eyes open and bulging
Death standing near
Knowing he will soon be indulging

No pulse, no rhythm
This situation is grim

Family is called
We are almost there
I hope you understand
How dearly we care

The pounding continues
Ribs made to fine powder
His heart remains quiet
But ours are much louder

The inevitable approaches
Too long we delayed
A time of death noted
A decision is made

A scream from outside
A wish to carry on
Family now here
But he is long gone

We tried our best
Our efforts superfluous
I hope he felt nothing
And I hope he forgives us

Life can be mean.

31
Insanity

I woke up on the same side of the bed
How could I expect today to be any different?

The same conversations
The same actions
The same mistakes
The same results

I woke up on the same side of the bed
How could I expect today to be any different?

The same conversations
The same actions
The same mistakes
The same results

I woke up on the same side of the bed
Perhaps today will be different.

32
Life's Unforgiving Rage

You dare defy me
Do you know who I am?
You dare question me
Don't look the other way.

I'll tear out your guts
From where you stand.
Now get out of the way
Nothing stands in mine.

Cower in the corner
Tremble with your tears.
Nothing can save you
For I am here.

You want love
I'll bring you pain.
It's sad but true
I'm here for you.

33
Pandemic of Panic

We hold our breath
As an invisible force preys on humanity
And as we are
Another unseen presence has emerged...

Panic
Begins to fester just beneath the skin's surface
Ready to spread like disease
Lie in wait for something as simple as...

A single look
A single word
A single action
Just enough to tip the scales...

Hysteria.
Grips the nation
Grips the world
Feeding the beast that spreads among us.

Can we stop the spread of one?
Or will they unite to destroy us?

34
Anger Builds

Anger builds
At first, collectively delicate, selectively effective
Advancing carefully to get to the objective

Before the sediment builds to obstruct the flow
For which the rage that exits with such great gusto
No one left to veto what was left to outgrow
Can no longer be tamed and must be let go

Upon to thee in the warpath
Unrelenting wrath and discontentment
With resentment til the aftermath

Relentment...

Left alone

Empty

Anger builds...

35
Without Pain, Would We Know?

To live without pain
    Without refrain

To live without sorrow
    Never fearing tomorrow

Would this be heaven?

Or…

Without pain
    Would life remain the same
    Unchanged whether sun or rain

Without sorrow
    Who cares about tomorrow
    With more time to borrow

Guiding others... without a compass.

36
The Gift

It's a blessing and a burden
What you have passed on to me
A chance to touch the lives of many
Most you already lightened plenty

For many years you cared for them
They grew older and so did you
Now you pass your torch to me
Enjoy more time to drink your tea.

Your presence towers over
Despite me being a foot taller
These shoes seem much too large
I'll have to figure out how to stay in charge

You have told me to tell them "patience"
But I think it is I that needs the same
They hang on to your presence
I'll have to set new precedents

I don't know what you saw in me
But I think they are beginning to see it too
And with this I will do my best
So from here I'll take care of all the rest.

37
Sitting on the Beach

I do not know what I am waiting for,
staring emptily out at the horizon.
The waves continue to crash, distracting
my eyes as I look out to sea, waiting
for it to give me answers. I feel
the grains of sand slip through
my grasp, though some decide
to linger, clinging to the sweat
of my palms. Though the ones I wish
to hold, slip away. The horizon is empty,
yet filled with color and concealed life.
An occasional flock of ravenous
gulls persistently dive, uninterested
in my presence, desperately
trying to secure their place. Comfort
from warm breeze turns to uncertainty,
as cool gusts foretell rain. Thunder confirms
an afternoon squall. It is almost time
to leave. I shiver, anxious
and excited. The electricity in the air
energizes and motivates halted gears
to turn. I prepare for the coming storm.
Waves crash ashore, awakening
me from slumber. I stand and walk
the shore carving a new path, soon
washed away by the tireless force. How
will others know to follow?

38

One Last Time, One More Time

You stand before me, a pack in hand. "One last cigarette," you tell yourself for the thousandth time. You saw your parents fade away to diseases of the lung. Yet you still prefer company with your coffee and beer. Each layer of clothing carries your ashen scent. "Today is the day." *See you again tomorrow.*

39

The Third Law

Waxing, waning
halted training.
Muscles soften
much too often.

A focus on others
soon enough it smothers.
The mind tends to follow
With too much to swallow.

But the soul is nourished
See how they have flourished?
A desire to do more.
So many to care for.

But every action without refrain, leads to strain.
Balancing reaction to remain, both strong and sane.

40
A Little Less Peanut Butter

I've told you before
Eat less peanut butter
But I know you won't change
And you know I won't change

We talk about what's right
We talk about what's wrong
I tell you how to fix the wrong
You listen to what is already right

You know you won't change
I know you won't change

I tell you to exercise
You tell me your joints hurt too much
I tell you to eat better
You tell me peanut butter tastes too good
I tell you to take medications
You tell me they are too expensive
We talk of the weather
At least we can agree on that

While I may not prolong your life
I can tell myself I have tried
And believe me I have
But at least I can be your friend

You tell me of your past jobs
And your favorite tv shows
You tell me of your family
And your lovely dog

I have not fixed you
But you seem to leave happier... And so do I
Perhaps you'll think of me tomorrow,
and eat just a little less peanut butter.

T.L. Larson

Learning to move on.

41
Procrastination

If there ever was a day...
If there ever was a way...

Has there...?
Is there...?

Yes... there have been days
Yes... there have been ways

Yet it remains to be done.

42
Always Tomorrow

If you say to me tomorrow
Run away with me, leave this all behind
Let the world show us what life truly is.
Would I have the courage to join?

Would I...?
Maybe tomorrow...

If I say to you tomorrow
Come with me on a journey to nowhere
Where we can follow dreams we never knew we had.
Would you cast away responsibility to follow?

Would you...?
Always tomorrow...

If we say again tomorrow
Let us live within this life
Wander with each other and breathe new life.
Would we decide to take a leap of faith?

Would we...?
Never today...

Alas, tomorrow always comes
And today we always stay

Maybe tomorrow...
Always tomorrow...
Never today...

43
An Acquaintance with Death

In the past,
I did not expect
To make such an acquaintance
With Death.

Yet, over the years
He has been one too frequent.
I now know he is one who wears many faces
And he is as ruthless as he is kind.

At times
I even found myself fascinated by his ways,
On the occasions
When he decided it was time for a visit

Taking those whose time had come
Never relenting
He came and he went
Just as the wind… or perhaps a final breath.

Sometimes in a simple story I happened to overhear
Sometimes for those I tried to save
Sometimes even for family or a friend

Sometimes expecting him
I prepared for his arrival
Sometimes surprising us
I reluctantly accepted his presence

And on occasion
Sometimes he rewarded us
Granting a beautiful departure
I would offer my thanks

Do not mistake our acquaintance though
He is no friend of mine
No… only an acquaintance
And still one I seldom understand.

And I do fear one day he will arrive for me
But coming to know his ways
I will accept his hand
And hopefully he will be my friend.

44
Posture and Attitude

When I first met you
I was younger
Just beginning to learn the true world of medicine
Starting to learn the things that no textbooks could teach

When I first met you
You were older
You had managed to outlive your death clock
But you remained with such great posture and attitude

Now I have aged (only some… thank you very much)
But your aging has halted…

When I first met you
I learned of a death sentence previously given
A diagnosis of metastatic lung cancer
One with rather poor prognosis

But your time was already served
And you still here despite
Standing before me…
A woman full of posture and attitude

You somehow outlasted your soul mate
Who then was waiting patiently for you
Knowing one day you would be reunited
And likely one day soon

You accepted your fate
And greeted death with such posture and attitude
He perhaps decided to let you stay
And grace the world a little longer

Perhaps if only to teach one more young doctor in training
And encourage him to work on his posture and attitude

As time passed, I saw you wither
The weight slid at first
Bones became more prominent
As you started to have difficulty swallowing

But through it all
You always remained with great posture and attitude

When I first met you
You stood so proud
When I said goodbye
You lay so peaceful

Like your mother told you, and you passed on to me
Each day is a blessing and a challenge
And good posture and positive attitude
Can get you where you need to be

I must admit… I still don't have great posture
And my attitude needs adjusting on occasion
But when I think of you
I stand a little taller and act a little kinder.

45
Forward

Just keep moving

Don't stop

For you might not restart

Just keep going

Just for fun.

46
Cursed

Madness...
ever since I've returned.

A journey from afar, led to groundbreaking discovery.
Yet here we are, too far from any hope of recovery.

We should have turned back,
for it all started to crack.
Pushed against the locals will,
only for a simple thrill.

A burial ground and broken taboo,
stumbled upon by me and my crew.
We scoffed at superstitions.
Hmph... such terrible decisions.

Could we be cursed from this tomb?
Why yes! I must now assume.
For now, I slip into madness,
as the world slips from its axis.

I only wish I could sleep,
but something terrible begins to creep
every time I close my eyes,
I can only lay and agonize.

For before these dry, red eyes
is something my imagination could not devise.
A ghastly, monstrous face appears,
this being straight from our worst fears.

A face of death and decay
taunting to take me away.
Its eyes almost unseeing,
my mind wishing itself unbeing.

As time passes it only moves
closer...
and closer...
Creeping ever so closer.

I try to fight to stay awake,
but I soon may find by mistake.
That I have slipped off and let go,
for with each second, heavier my eyes grow.

Even now I still see the hideous face.
I've no thoughts on how to efface
this tormenting face from appearing
in the mirror,
in the shadows,
waiting for me in the darkness...

47

Drums

My hi-hat is off to you,
as the rhythm of my day is thrown off.
Too stuck into one rhythm,
I've been snared.

The cymbal crashes.
My eyes widen.
You have my attention,
as the base within my chest gains tempo.

48
Grip

Summer time triumphs,
freedom of no school breathes new life
into the young spirit, as well as the old
one who desires a break.
Time spent together, canoeing
into unfamiliar territory.
No fear. Trusting
in each other.
The man aged by time
and sun, smothers the paddle with
bear-like hands. A grip so strong,
new grooves begin to form. The stroke
flusters the water, creating
its own current and waves.
The boy growing, quiet
and curious, gently wraps his fingers
around the grip. Each dip in the water
allows the paddle to almost slip out into
the water hardly disturbed
by his movements.
The boy learns strength
and thickens his skin. His paddle moving
with more direction.
The man relearns to understand,
lightens his grip and slows down. Yearning
for more time.
The canoe cuts through the water
and together they arrive.

49
The Evolution of a Man

The boy
So innocent
Curious about the world

The young adolescent
Stumbles through change
Attempting to find identity

The late teenager
Rebellious for attention
Yearning for freedom of choice

The young man
Invincible from the world
Desires to conquer all

The career man
Ambitious to bring change
Frustrated with a world that refuses

The family man
Softens a hardened heart
Accepting the world that is his

The elder man
Wise in the way of life
Desires to teach those who'll listen

The dying man
Debates from within
Accepting of fate or questioning life's choices

The deceased man
Remembered for his greatness
Finds rest

Goodbye for now...

50
An Incomplete Farewell

(an incomplete Sestina)

New beginnings are around the corner, waiting...
But that means I must soon say farewell.
And saying goodbye is rarely painless,
Especially when leaving those you admire.
I am blessed to have new friends and family,
but I don't know how to begin my goodbye.

So I must now begin this dance to say goodbye...
For unfortunately, I have other engagements waiting.
I will soon move on to be with other family.
So again, I *must* say farewell
But maybe I can stay a bit longer with those I admire
Though leaving now without a word would be painless.

I am tempted for it to be painless
For it really is so hard to say goodbye
Never knowing the next time I will see those I admire.
Alas, I have drug my feet and kept you waiting
So here goes my farewell
One final song to my family...

Farewell for now.

- T.L. Larson

It has been a journey to get here, and I know I am only just beginning to scratch the surface. I feel I will have much more to say, if there are those interested in listening.

A special thank you to all those who have helped get me to where I am today.

A *very* special thank you to my wonderful parents.
It is because of you that I am here. But not only that. You were our heroes and role models growing up. You are why we try to be the best people we can.

Another thank you to all the wonderful doctors and teachers who have taught me and influenced me not only as a practitioner, but as a human being. I desire to list you all, but a very special thanks to:

    Dr. Dennis Mayeaux
    Dr. Dennis Saver
    Dr. Rene Loyola
    Dr. Mark Knudson
    Dr. Aubry Koehler

And to you the reader, thank you!

Thank you for taking the time to read this book!

I truly hope you found something you connected with and enjoyed.

If you indeed did enjoy this one, keep an eye out for part 2 to come out sometime in mid to late 2021.

A Break from the Chaos has literally been my break from the chaos. It is my safe space to come and vent, breathe, and place random thoughts.

It is and has been a constant work in progress. I expect I will release the final product in 2 to 4 volumes, depending on how well the writing spirit keeps up.

Made in the USA
Columbia, SC
17 December 2020